Photographic Memory

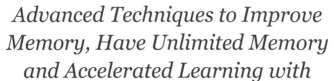

*Advanced Techniques to Improve
Memory, Have Unlimited Memory
and Accelerated Learning with
Memory Techniques*

Logan G Davidson

expressed written consent of the Publisher. All additional rights are reserved.

The information in the following pages is broadly considered to be a truthful and accurate account of facts, and as such any inattention, use or misuse of the information in question by the reader will render any resulting actions solely under their purview. There are no scenarios in which the publisher or the original author of this work can be in any fashion deemed liable for any hardship or damages that may befall them after undertaking information described herein.

Additionally, the information found on the following pages is intended for informational purposes only and should thus be considered, universal. As befitting its nature, the information presented is without assurance regarding its continued validity or interim quality. Trademarks that mentioned are done without written consent and can in no way be considered an endorsement from the trademark holder.

Your Free Gift

As a way of saying thank you for your purchase, I wanted to offer you a free bonus E-book called **5 Incredible Hypnotic Words To Influence Anyone**

Download the free guide here: https://www.subscribepage.com/b1b5i8

If your trying to persuade or influence other people then words are the most important tool you have to master.

As Humans we interact with words, we shape the way we think through words, we express ourselves through words. Words evoke feelings and have the ability to talk to the lister's subconscious.

In this free guide, you'll discover 5 insanely effective words that you can easily use to start hypnotizing anyone in conversation.

Listen to this book for free

Do you want to be able to listen to this book whenever you want? Maybe whilst driving to work or running errands. It can be difficult nowadays to sit down and listen to a book. So I am really excited to let you know that this book is available in audio format. What's great is you can get this book for FREE as part of a 30-day audible trial. Thereafter if you don't want to stay an Audible member you can cancel, but keep the book.

Benefits of signing up to audible:
- After the trial, you get 1 free audiobook and 2 free audio originals each month
- Can roll over any unused credits
- Choose from over 425,000 + titles
- Listen anywhere with the Audible app and across multiple devices
- Keep your audiobooks forever, even if you cancel your membership

Click below to get started
Audible US - https://tinyurl.com/y4pgu8g2
Audible UK - https://tinyurl.com/yyxvyh9a
Audible FR - https://tinyurl.com/y6t28q6o
Audible DE - https://tinyurl.com/yy8h8v7t

Table of Contents

Introduction

Welcome and thank you for purchasing *Photographic Memory* to hone your brain's unused skill sets!

It's 2 AM on a Wednesday night, and you're still studying. You are on your third mug of tea, your eyes are starting to blur, and no matter *what* you do you just can't get the stuff you need to know for that test tomorrow morning to stick. Wouldn't it be nice if you had a photographic memory? Then all you would have to do is read everything once. On the day of the test, you would be able to mentally pull up the page the important stuff was on, and like magic, all the info you need would be there. You would ace that test and ride off into the sunset.

Okay, I love metaphors, but the point is that the phrase photographic memory sounds a little bit like a magician's trick or a Hollywood cliché, well, because it is. Pop culture from celebrities to movies have used photographic memory to spice up storylines for years, but no one truly has it. When we talk about photographic memory, we refer to those who can look at something, take a mental snapshot, and later remember every single detail perfectly. That snapshot might be so good that the person notices something they didn't see before. The thing is, *no one* has *this kind* of memory.

However, there are multitudes of ways that you can strengthen your brainpower to help you with those overwhelming tests, to remember details of recent events, and much more! There are techniques, tricks, and methods that you can use to harness your brain's power and use it to your advantage in many aspects of life.

In this book, you are going to discover:

- All the basics you need to know to understand what photographic memory is;

- How this kind of memory works;

- All the disbeliefs that surround the topic;

- The benefits of honing a better memory;

- How to develop a better memory with revision reading;

- What memory chunking is and why it is essential for better memory;

- How to use mnemonics to improve your memory;

- Memory techniques and tricks; and

- What it is like to live in the shoes of those with a highly engaged memory.

There is an entire world of possibility out there that has yet to be uncovered by you! Every effort has been made to ensure that this book is full of as much useful information as possible, please enjoy!

Chapter 1:
The Basics of Photographic Memory

What is photographic memory?

'Photographic memory' is referred to by the scientific communities as "*eidetic memory*". The word '*eidetic*' derives from the Greek word that means "*seen*".

Those that harness photographic memory skills can visually recall information in great detail. Those with photographic memory are capable of taking and absorbing memory snapshots and remembering them without error. While both phrases can be utilized interchangeably, they each have their own differences:

- Photographic memory refers to the ability to view and recall things in your memory

- Eidetic memory refers to the capability to remember numbers and/or text

What is eidetic memory?

Most human beings have bursts of eidetic memory from time to time, also referred to as 'sporadic eidetic memory.'

Have you ever had a negative experience that you can recall in such detail that you could reach out and touch it? Being able to remember events in this kind of detail is an example of this type of memory. It's still not proven if this type of memorization is trainable since it shows up in individuals who go through events that impact them deeply.

It seems like a superpower that is too good to be true, right? It most certainly does. Therefore, scientists and average people have a hard time believing in its true relevancy.

Factors that contribute to photographic memory

How can one inherit this skill? According to science, there are a few key factors that play into creating a photographic mind:

- *Genetics* play an important role in determining our memory's capacity. Some are naturally born with eidetic memory, and the rest is how we utilize our brain, train it, and develop it over time.

- *Lifestyle* choices are essential to maximizing your brain's ultimate health. You must have a quality sleep, exercise, a good diet, and proper stimulation to create an environment for your brain to grow those memory cells and enhance cognition.

- Establishing a *training* program is needed to unlock your brain's potential. This involves using photographic memory methods that help to mold your mind into a memory machine.

The truth is, *everyone* can develop a memory that resembles photographic recollection when they use the right tools and methods. Some people are born with unique brain chemistries that help them to become experts in eidetic memory, but anyone can do simple things to exponentially improve their memory. It is all about taking the proper steps towards your goals and adopting a healthy lifestyle that caters to great brain health and capacity.

The beautiful human brain and memory

Our brains go through a lot of core developmental changes, which is when people have reported having the capabilities of a photographic memory the most. While most of us are equipped with some memory capability naturally, those with photographic memory can recall very specific information about certain experiences and everyday life.

Many of us have more of an eidetic rather than photographic memory. Our memories are more like a puzzle rather than a photograph itself. To correctly recall past events, we must piece together all aspects of that memory. As humans, we are great at remembering the main idea of what occurred, but leave out other details, like the colors on the walls or the furniture in the room, etc.

Memory is a very complex process that many scientists have yet to 100 percent understand. What they *do* know is that when we live through experiences, the hippocampus and frontal cortex sections of our brains make a decision about what parts of the situation are worth retaining and which are not. Tiny pieces of all situations are stored within many parts of our brain and then reassembled at the time they need to be recalled. This is why we are unable to remember every single detail.

Imagine there are many little desks within your brain and there is a secretary assigned to each one. When we experience something, our brain chooses what to remember and then gives a portion of those memories to each secretary, who store them in their own file cabinet for safe keeping. Sometimes, our brains cannot remember some details, even if they are pertinent. This is because it cannot recall all the little secretaries that it dropped pieces of information to. Our brains do, however, do a pretty great job at cataloging the crucial areas that it knows we will need to recall later.

It might be simpler to view those with photographic memory as if their minds are wired differently from rest of the population. The traces of elements within a memory that we long forgot about are lurking within the brain for days, months, and even years. There are so many common misconceptions about photographic memory to begin with, and the phenomenon is so rare that it actually looks rather fake. This is due to the fact that it is a direct result of genetic mutations that are quite uncommon. To be able to further study and peer inside the minds of those with such a talent is difficult. Scientists have to in some way find these individuals to be able to run more tests and gather further evidence that can wipe out those myths.

Often, we all have photographic skills that are heavily present during the first few years of our childhood, while our brains are going through foundational developmental changes. As we become adults, we tend to use specific areas of our brain, rather than being able to utilize them all. To develop habits that fuel our memory abilities that we are born with is how we learn and acquire knowledge that will feed our later skill sets when it comes to remembering.

Scientists have studied children for decades as they attempt to crack the code behind this type of memory. With so few adults exhibiting these sorts of behaviors, it is difficult to tell what clear-cut factors play a role in assisting those with a photographic memory.

Renowned People with Photographic Memory

Rachmaninov

This man is a compelling composer who possessed the type of eidetic memory to recall musical notes at an alarming speed. There were many Russians who gave this gentleman extremely complicated musical pieces to memorize. He would have them down pat one to two days later, depending on the length of the piece.

Mr. T

Yes indeed, we are speaking of *the* Mr. T! This African-American man claims that he did not have to do a whole lot of studying growing up due to his skills in memorizing things. He states that he spent much of his time during school hours doodling or staring out the schoolhouse windows while daydreaming.

Ferdinand Marcos

As the president of the Philippines, this man was noted to have a fantastic memory, especially when it came to writing down the details of Imelda's shoes.

Jerry Lucas

Playing from the 1950's throughout the 1970's, Lucas has been named one of the top 50 players in basketball history. He is best known for writing 60+ books based on his ability to recall alone. He spends his time now traveling the world and educating people on the memory-retention system that he created. I have no doubt that Lucas does not need lecture notes while giving them!

Guillermo del Toro

This man directed the films Pan's Labyrinth and Haunted Mansion. It has been said to have a grand photographic memory, which would explain why his films are so virtually intriguing.

Teddy Roosevelt

Our past president of the grand old United States could recite, word for word, newspaper articles and large portions of books he read. He was a renowned speed reader who is reported to have read 2-3 books PER day.

Chapter 1: The Basics of Photographic Memory

Tesla

This man had no issue reciting entire books, but also stated that he encountered very random and blinding depictions of light that were paired with hallucinations. He had the capability to go back in time within his mind, recalling distinct details of very early portions of his childhood.

Photographic memory is a blessing in disguise. Being able to recall numbers, words, names and other images and information with accuracy is quite a skill. These types of abilities are caused by the process of neuroplasticity within our brain, which provides us the capability of creating new connections by the breaking down of old ones.

Some people are naturally born with these abilities, while many others must practice and use particular techniques to sharpen their memories. The remaining chapters of this book will cover, in detail, some great tips and other vital information you need to know to get yourself on the right track; perhaps to someday remember this entire book!

Photographic Memory

"*Everyone has a photographic memory, some just don't have film.*"

This quote is very true when it comes to understanding those who exhibit photographic memory. While research has been unable to find much valuable information or resources to verifying this way of remembering, there are certainly plenty of people ready to vouch for its certainty.

Chapter 2:
How Memory Works

Memory helps make us who we are, whether recognizing loved ones, recalling past joys, or just remembering how to walk and talk and fry an egg. Memory is the chain that connects our past to our present; if it breaks, we are left untethered and incapable of either leaving the present moment or embrace the future.

Memory isn't an all-or-nothing thing. Some memories can be processed automatically, and they are stored differently than your personal or factual memories, such as your first kiss or how to recite math equations or who won the Cold War.

Technically speaking, memory is learning that has persisted over time. It is information that has been stored and can be recalled. During situations like remembering information during an exam, our brains' recollection system works in 3 different ways: through recall, recognition, and relearning. If you think back to all the kinds of tests you have taken during school, they're all designed to evaluate how you access stored information in these ways.

Recall is how you reach back into your mind and bring up information, just as you do on fill in the blanks on a test. So, if I say _____ is the capital of Greece, your brain hopefully will recall that the answer is Athens.

Recognition is more like a multiple-choice test. You only need to identify old information when presented with it, such as:

- o Which of the following was not an ancient city in Greece?

    - Athens

    - Marathon

    - _Pompeii_

    - Sparta

Relearning is sort of like refreshing or reinforcing old information. When you study for a final exam, you relearn things you half-forgotten more easily than you did when you were first learning them, such as a basic timeline of the Greek Empire.

The stages of storing information

But *how?* How does all that data that were exposed to all the time every day become memory? In the late 1960s, American psychologists Richard Atkinson and Richard Shiffrin figured out the basics of memory enough to break it into three stages:

First, it is *encoded* into the brain, then *stored* for future use and then eventually *retrieved*. Sounds simple, right? By now, you may have figured out that just because you take a lot of stuff about your mind for granted doesn't mean that it is not complicated.

Atkinson and Shiffrin's model refers to recording things we want to remember as an immediate but fleeting sensory memory. If you do recall something after seeing it for just a few seconds, it's because you successfully managed to shuffle it into your short-term memory where you probably encoded it through rehearsal. This is how you briefly remember things like phone numbers and passwords.

However, this information only stays in your short-term memory for under 30 seconds without a lot of rehearsal. Unless you repeat those small chunks of information repeatedly, you are likely to forget it quickly since your mind, amazing as it is, can only store 4 to 7 distinct bits of information at a time, to where it gets erased or stored into long-term memory.

Long-term memory

Long-term memory is like a durable and ridiculously spacious storage unit, holding all your knowledge skills and experiences. Since the days of Atkinson and Shriffin, psychologists have recognized that the classical definition of short-term memory didn't capture all the processes involved in the transfer of information to your long-term memory.

Later generations of psychologists revisited the whole idea of short-term memory and updated it to the more comprehensive concept of *working memory*.

Working memory

Working memory involves *all* the ways that we take short-term information and stash it in our long-term stores. Increasingly we think of it as involving both explicit and implicit processes. Those ways are:

- Visual-spatial information

- Central executive

- Auditory rehearsal

Explicit memory

When we store information consciously and actively that's an explicit process. We make the most of this after the working memory when we study so that we can know that Athens is the capital of Greece, Pompeii was a Roman town and not a Greek one, for example.

We capture facts and knowledge that we think we're going to need. Like when you are told to remember something specific like a name or number, you concentrate on that detail and file it away, even if just for a brief time.

Implicit memory

We are not conscious of *everything* we take in, but our working memory often transfers stuff we're not aware of to the long-term storage. We call this an implicit process, the kind you don't have to actively concentrate on.

A good example might be a classically conditioned association; if you get all sweaty and nervous at the dentist because you had a root canal last year. You don't *need* to pull up that file in your brain on the last time you got your face drilled down to think, "<u>Oh, oral surgery. NOT my favorite</u>." The implicit process covers all this automatically.

Automatic Processing

All types of automatic processing are hard to shut off. Unless you have something unusual going on in your brain, you might not have much choice but to learn this way. For instance, the way you learned to not put your hand into a fire. That learning would have happened automatically as soon as you first yank your hand away from an open flame.

Whether those things are locked explicitly or implicitly or both, they are different kinds of long-term memory.

Procedural Memory

Procedural memory refers to how we remember to do things, such as riding a bike or reading. It's difficult to learn at first but eventually, you can do without thinking about it.

Episodic memory

Long-term memory can also be episodic, tied to specific episodes in your life, such as remembering that time that Grace fell out of her chair in chemistry, and everybody started laughing uncontrollably.

There are other kinds of long-term memory too. We are continuously learning about the psychology of the whole complex phenomenon.

Tricks for Healthy Memory

For healthy memories, there are all sorts of tricks to help you improve your memory capabilities.

Mnemonics help with memorization, and I'm sure you know a few that take the form of acronyms, such as:

- ROY G. BIV for the colors of the rainbow

Mnemonics work, in part, by organizing items into familiar manageable units with a process called _chunking_. For example, it may be hard to recall a number with 7 digits, but it is much easier to commit to memory in the rhythm of a phone number.

Strategies like mnemonics and chunking can help you with explicit processes but _how_ well you retain your data can depend on how deep you dig through the different levels of processing.

Shallow processing

Shallow processing lets you encode information on basic auditory or visual levels based on the sound, structure, or appearance of a word.

Deep processing

To really retain information, you must activate your deep processing, which allows you to encode semantically based on actual meanings associated with the word.

If you really want to make information stick in your mind, you will want to connect it to something meaningful or related to your own personal emotional experience. How much information you encode and remember depends on both the time you took to learn it and how you made it personally relevant to you.

Memory is extremely powerful. It's constantly shaping and reshaping your brain, your life, and your identity. Our memories either haunt us or sustain us, but either way, they define us. Without them, we are left to wander alone in the dark.

Chapter 3:
Debunking Photographic
Memory Myths

The ultimate questions of photographic and eidetic memory have yet to be 100 percent proven by science, which makes it difficult to decipher if people truly possess these abilities or if they are just awesome at retaining information and memory more naturally than others. Because of this lack of proof, there are several myths around the idea of photographic memory, which we will be debunking in this chapter.

The Most Common Myths about Photographic Memory

Photographic memory works just like a camera

If only! You would be surprised at the number of people who truly think that this kind of memory works just like a camera; a simple 'click!' and you have captured information forever! Perhaps this can be a futuristic idea, but photographic memory, unfortunately, doesn't work this way.

The decline of remembering information occurs gradually

Forgetting details of a piece of information or a specific event often happens right after it has occurred. If you fail to take those details away with you from that experience, that piece of information will be lost within your mind for eternity. Even those that possess aspects of a photographic memory don't have the power to remember things they choose to block out.

Confidence is an indicator of having a great memory

Naturally, when you can remember more information that the person beside you at the drop of a hat, you are going to get a nice stroke to your self-confidence. But confidence should not be the ultimate sign that someone has a great memory.

Events that are emotional result in accurate memories

Traumatic experiences can be revisited in the future in vivid details, but those memories can just as easily be eliminated from your mind as well. This goes for any type of event that you have endured that falls into the stressful category.

Negative memories can be buried and recovered later in life

Many people believe that negative memories can be repressed for some time and that they can be buried for eternity. It is also believed that even though memories may be buried, that they can be dug back up with the help of a psychologist or hypnotist. This myth depends on the individual.

Some wish to repress their memories, and others wish to unbury them to later cope and move forward with their lives. No matter what, people who have been abused mentally, physically or emotionally, will always have some recollection, no matter how much effort goes into deeply burying those memories.

Memory is a "thing"

Many folks think that their memory is an object that they can pick up, warp and mold to their liking. You cannot say that one part of your memories is "healthier" than others.

Memory is a process and should be viewed as an activity. Just like activities that you perform throughout everyday life, you may recall things in a good or bad fashion. Recalling things more easily takes practice and skill, "practice makes perfect."

Memories are only stored in one area of the human brain

False! There is not *one* place in the human brain that is responsible for storing all our recollections. Individual pieces of our memories are created from tiny fragments of memories that occur over time.

The memory process is built up of a complex integration of many different factors. All our memories are stored in various methods and placed within different areas of the brain. Even similar kinds of memories are recalled in various ways.

There is a secret in becoming a master at recall

Sadly, there is no secret that critics are keeping on the topic of recollection. Different methods of improving your memory depend on what works best for the individual. There are lots of various memory skills to improve memorizing different types of information. Many of those methods have been around for as much as 2,000 years.

There is no quick way to improve your memory, but you can learn more about the way you learn and retain information by utilizing different kinds of methods. If one doesn't work well for you, try another! What do you have to lose?

There are "easy" ways to memorize

People who are looking to enhance their memorization skills look for the easy ticket to the train of expertise. They think by learning one trick they will then be able to master photographic memory. Those with this mindset end up very disappointed. *Memorization is a* _learned skill_. There is no "easy" way to go about it. There are many variables that go into becoming a great driver. The same goes with acquiring memorizing skills, it requires some effort on your part to get the most out of it.

You are stuck with your negative memories forever

Picture memory as a cardboard box; Those with a good memory have a bigger box, and those with weaker memories have a smaller box. As we acquire a new skill set, it is written on a piece of paper. Those with the bigger box throw in the papers, while the one with a smaller box must take the time to place each piece of paper nice and neat inside their box.

Even though the person with the weaker natural memory has a smaller box, theirs is more organized, making it much easier to recall information. This entire box metaphor debunks this theory that you will be stuck with your bad memories.

Hypnosis can retrieve lost memories

It is heavily believed that everything we see and experience is stored deep inside our brain. We believe that there is a method to reach it, the idea of hypnosis being a popular one. Sadly, hypnosis rarely ever aids in proper recollection, but rather has the potential to harm our faith in memorization.

Having amnesia means you forget everything, including your identity

We have all seen at least one or more movies that suggest that those who suffer from amnesia have forgotten all their past life. Realistically, amnesia is caused by illness or damage to vital areas of the brain that make it sometimes impossible to collect and store new memories.

With certain degrees of amnesia, it is difficult, if not impossible, to create short-term memories from long-term ones. Those that suffer in real life can easily recall past stories but are never able to tell you what they wore, did or consumed that same day.

Some people possess natural photographic memories

It is unlikely that anyone has the memorization skill set of a robot. When people undergo memory tests, they are likely utilizing memory skills to recall information. People mistake photographic memories with the mere practice of memorization techniques. So, in other words, if you take the time to learn photographic skills, you too can be just as sharp as those that claim they do!

You only have a certain period to hone your memorization skills

You are *never* too old to learn! While it is true that the older you get, the more difficult it can be to remember, older people who utilize memory skills often can remember just as much as an average 20-year-old. No matter the age, a human being has quite the capability to learn and process information.

Memorizing things constantly helps to boost memory

Memorizing things repeatedly will not create a brain that is better able to memorize. If you practice memorizing skills instead of attempting to always memorize a certain set of information you will improve your overall memory. Period.

Those with trained memories never forget

Even if you dedicate yourself to practicing photographic memorization skills, it doesn't mean you will remember everything. An ironic aspect about the human brain is that it tends to remember things it *wants* to recall. No matter how many memorization skills you learn, you are going to still forget some things. However, you will be able to recall things much easier and clearer than you used to.

Memorizing too much clutters the mind

Think back to the box analogy we used earlier; recalling doesn't depend on how much information you can soak up and retain. It depends on how well you mentally organize the information you acquire.

That's why it is essential to keep the things you want to recall organized and easy to mentally find. The capacity that our brains have is boundless; the more we learn, the easier it is for our minds to retain that new incoming information.

Only 10% of the brain is utilized by most people

There is not a single way to measure brain power that scientists have agreed to use, meaning no one knows how much of the brain we use. However, it is true that many of us fail to use our brains to their fullest potential. This is why memory training and brain expanding activities are essential in keeping a healthy mind. By learning memory skills, we can boost our brain power and improve our memory if we decide to take the initiative to do such.

Chapter 4:
Unknown Facts about
Photographic Memory

Photographic memory has been used as an excuse

Those blessed with higher terms of memory retention have used their gift as an excuse when they have knowingly screwed up during writing assignments, plagiarizing content that they supposedly "memorized" and then used by accident.

Exceptional memory is seen many times with disabilities

Individuals with mental disabilities, such as Down's syndrome, have been shown to harness amazing memorization skills. If you remember the movie Rain Man, it was based on a real-life man named Kim Peek. It was said that he read and could recall every page of 9,000 different books he had read in his lifetime. This type of memory greatly surpasses a regular human being's mental capabilities when it comes to retaining that kind of information.

Good memories are good for a reason

Those that possess phenomenal memorization skills and techniques typically can only be that amazing at retaining and recalling information from just one subject area most of the time.

The more time you spend 'exercising' your brain, the better it performs

Our brains are just like muscles and can become 'buff' over time. The more time you take to mentally exercise your mind, the more connections you can form from cell to cell within your brain. The more connections there are, the more brain power you have to retain and later recall information.

Some memorization skills are gifts, while some take practice

Children who possess the abilities of an eidetic memory are naturally born with it. Some scholars exhibit phenomenal memory naturally, too. There is nothing others can do to acquire those abilities to the levels in which these special people have. But there are many who have great memorization thanks to their dedicated time and disciplined practice.

Eidetic memory is mostly found in children

Scientists are still unsure why there are more children than adults that have eidetic abilities. At about age six or seven, these capabilities begin to fade. This is due to childhood development. Our brains must be able to filter out unimportant information to function efficiently and effectively. Having all that data packed in our brains as a child who notices all sorts of details throughout their day can greatly hinder being able to have a functional and good working memorization.

Eidetic memory is not perfect

Even those that possess the ability to recall sequences of letters or numbers are never perfect 100 percent of the time. The accuracy greatly declines after a matter of just a few minutes.

There are mental abilities that mimic photographic memory

Those that claim that they have photographic memory perform in ways that mimic the greater aspects of this type of brain functioning. Some scholars can recall loads of information while teaching a class or writing a biography. Some people are skilled in the use of mnemonic devices. Other people really do have a good sense of an eidetic memory. But no one really has a profound photographic memory.

Chapter 5:
Benefits of Developing a
Photographic Memory

Have you noticed that there are people in the world around you that are confident, intelligent, and successful? They likely have developed their photographic memory to an enhanced state. It doesn't mean that these people are more intelligent than we are, they just have a skill set that we have yet to master.

How is it that the successful people seem to have success in many aspects of their lives? When I was at school, there were students who would easily breeze through tests and didn't seem to have the stress of studying like the rest of us.

When I joined the workforce, there would be colleagues who would give presentations with ease and poise. These people were accurate, had great attention to detail, were organized and very thorough. They would also have meaningful relationships that thrived.

It's a fact that what sets these people apart is their ability to memorize and then recall large amounts of information with ease. Superior intellect is not necessarily what these folks possess, but an ability for photographic memory whether developed and learned or naturally given.

The neural pathways in the brain become stronger when you develop your photographic memory, which opens more parts of the brain that may not have been used much before. Developing photographic memory increases your overall brain activity and brings benefits to many areas of your life, such as:

- Increased reading speed and comprehension

- Increased peripheral vision and awareness

- Greatly improved concentration and focus

Chapter 5: Benefits of Developing a Photographic Memory

All these things enable one to learn so much faster and more effectively, but it does take practice and discipline.

Once I realized the benefits to be gained from having a photographic memory, my journey began to find how I could develop this type of almost super-human power. It is thought that all of us are born with a photographic memory, but as we grow older, our habits stop us from using this skill. We can develop it again, thankfully, and reap the benefits it has on our lives. There are now a few courses that you can take to develop your photographic memory. Some start with a speed reading, but photographic memory is so much more than just a speed reading ability.

Benefits of Improved Memory

Better judge of character

Being able to judge character, especially when you are meeting new people, is essential. It can help you to assess facial expressions and people's posture correctly, which can help you to decide if you should socialize with them or avoid them.

When you start off in a new place, you can figure out right away and have all that information on good character memorized to easily determine who you should add to your group of friends and who you should avoid.

Ability to study with ease

Imagine having a test tomorrow and not having studied a second for it? Frightening, right? When you have a developed photographic memory, all you have to do is look through your notes and textbook information, and you are free to go about your life.

Ability to remember a lot more information

With a well-defined memory, you are better able to remember tiny details, from what someone wore on a certain day to exact layouts of obstacles courses, etc.

You can recall small details

With a photographic memory, you can notice details that many other folks often overlook.

Improved organization

With a better memory, you are better able to organize physically and mentally, meaning you can organize your thoughts and pertinent information in such a way that you can recall them later with ease., You are also better able to remember where physical items are, etc.

You can master intricate activities

If you have ever observed painters, you will notice that they do quite a bit of staring when looking at the subject they are painting. This is because they are trying to take in all those tiny details and get them as precise as they can. Those with eidetic memory can create portraits with just a few glances at a stranger.

Other Benefits

Have you ever stopped to think what really sets people apart? Throughout school, there was always that one student in the class that seemed to breeze through the toughest tests, while you sat there, trying to recall the answer to a certain question. There are those that can perform presentations with only a few minutes of preparation and some of us that take a week before the due date to just attempt to nail each word we wish to convey.

In the workplace, there are those that are almost always precise in their work, highly detailed and organized to a fault. These individuals also seemed to have the best relationships, remembering things about others that many of us would forget right after obtaining.

An important aspect of what sets people apart is their mere ability to memorize and recall with ease whatever they desire. These people are not necessarily superior to others with above-human powers, they simply possess photographic memory on different levels.

But what, in fact, is the point of taking the time to learn the ways of obtaining the amazing abilities of photographic memory? Within this chapter, you will gain insight into the many positives, as well as a few negatives, that inheriting photographic memory has to offer.

Stronger neural pathways

When you begin to develop enhanced memory, this opens up the doors to parts of your mind that you were not aware of before. There are many areas of our brains that never get used to their fullest potential, which is actually very unfortunate. Imagine what we could do if we all used every inch of our beautiful mind?

When you begin to really develop a better memory, you will notice:

- Increased activity in your brain that makes other aspects of your life better

- Faster reading speeds

- Ability to comprehend new information at a quick rate

- Improved concentration and focus

Able to recall small details with ease

When you create the capability to take in so much information all at once, you will consequently notice that you can recall details of experiences much better.

Cons of Improved Memory

Even the best things have a negative side to them:

Recalling things that you don't want to remember

Those with photographic memory recall and visualize things to the tiniest detail, even things they wish could otherwise be erased from their memory altogether. This includes things about people they may not even know personally but may have seen for only a matter of minutes.

Unable to control memories

There are some people who have the sort of memory that they are unable to control. For example, if one were sitting in math class learning a new lesson, they may remember every problem they acquired knowledge of previously regarding that same sort of lesson. This could tend to make one feel overwhelmed.

Recollections can take up tons of space in the brain

Just like the memory card of a camera eventually fills up and you have to delete some images to continue using it, our brains work the exact same way. Having hundreds of thousands of images and recollections of information flying around in your mind can cause it to become quite cluttered, which consumes a lot of mental energy and can create unnecessary stress, as well as a feeling of being overwhelmed.

Being misunderstood

Most people do not know and do not have a photographic memory, which means they are unable to relate to the way you view and absorb information. Some may even be alarmed by the way you can memorize certain things. If someone is staring at them to figure them out right off the bat, it is not a great ice-breaker at first, to say the least.

Recalling negative bad memories

Those with enhanced memory can recall precisely what their ex-significant other looked like when they broke up with them. They can remember the faces of the entire class when they embarrassed themselves. They will recall bloody images from movies and childhood wounds they received as a child.

Chapter 6:
Developing Memory for
Revision Reading

Exams are coming...three very scary words, right? And nothing will stop you from acing your tests like THE FOG. You know the feeling; you have read the same page over and over but the facts just won't stick in your mind. There is page after page of mind numbing notes you must get through, but how can you fit it all in? Before it all gets too overwhelming, remember, you are not alone and there are very simple things you can do to improve your memory!

The Different Types of Learning

First you need to find out what kind of learner you are. You can do this by seeing what characteristics match your learning style the most or try out multiple choice tests online. You could very well be a mix of different types. Once you know, you can start tailoring your revision accordingly.

- **Visual learners** are those who learn visually and prefer to see information and visualize the relationships between ideas being presented.

  o Do the best with graphics and charts and with highly visual presentations where one can easily see the relationships between various points.

- **Auditory learners** are those that prefer to hear information rather than see, visualize, or read it.

  o Do best by reciting the information aloud to remember it later

  o Need a chance to repeat points of information back to themselves or others in the form of questions or asking other people questions.

o   Set facts and pertinent information to rhythms you can easily remember.

- **Reading and writing learners** are those that learn the best by reading and/or writing information. This allows them to interact with the text, which is more powerful for them to memorize than hearing or seeing images.

    o   Do best with quizzes that provide them a chance to write down things they have learned.

    o   They like annotated handouts of presentations so that they can read along with the information being taught.

- **Kinesthetic learners** are those that prefer hands-on and experimental learning. They learn the best when they are doing something.

    o   Add exercises in with this type of learning so that they can move

> around and demonstrate information they have learned.
>
> o Get them to jot things down to remember them later as well.

All the above tips under each variation of learning will help you boost your memory's overall effectiveness. Those tips also help add meaning and context to what you're trying to learn. It's the restructuring and reorganizing that really makes you remember.

The good news? Once you started putting these techniques into practice, make sure to take a break. Resting after learning something new helps you remember it for longer! Exams might be coming, but guess what? You will be fine!

Chapter 7:
Strategies to Strengthen
Photographic Memory

C an you harness this human super-power for yourself? The answer is most often YES! You can easily learn how to remember more things in a clear frame of mind by just learning techniques and practicing them on a regular basis.

This chapter is full of unique strategies for those that struggle with retaining information to help learn the secrets of this skill, as well as tips and tricks for those that wish to further enhance their memory skills. Within this chapter, there are going to be several different techniques provided for beginners to experts.

Before we look at these strategies to a sharper mind, it is important to remember some of the fundamentals of what makes up memory itself:

- We remember things that stand out to us, things that are offensive, sexually driven, funny, or plain absurd.

- We are exceptional at recalling dimensional information, routes, and layouts.

- Our minds are naturally visual creatures, and it is the most common way we learn and retain information from the outside world.

The Memory Palace

If we look back in history, this method of memory enhancement was used by many of our ancestors starting in the 5th century. The term 'palace' plays a pertinent role in this method, so pay attention.

Are you going to need to remember those lecture notes to give that amazing speech in a few days? You can do it! View your memory as a hard drive that stores everything you have absorbed in your lifetime so far. Our brains are great at remembering some things but terrible at recalling others. It does not take much in any of the following methods in this chapter to get frustrated. The trick is, however, to work *with* your memory. When you get frustrated, you will work against it, which will leave you wandering for hours, never being able to recall those words that will capture your audience's attention.

Our great ancestors did not have to recall long lists but rather needed to recall things to survive. We thrived on hunting and gathering. Even though we did not need to memorize numbers or instructions, we still needed to remember where to search for food, and the quickest way to our shelters, as well as what plants not to eat and which foods provided the best nutrients.

It was from then on that we gradually became better and more apt to remembering less vital things through the means of visuals and spatial information. You are not alone if you struggle to recall your grocery list or phone numbers. Humans are not mentally graceful this way, but we are when it comes to remembering places. This is where the title of this technique comes in!

Memory experts have learned to not work against the brains' natural rhythms, but instead, work with them to set-up easy to recall formats. It is all about taking the memories we struggle to recall and turning them into the types of memories that our brains are equipped to handle. Remember those fundamentals mentioned previously? Here are the steps to mix them together to help you recall any kind of information!

Step One: Build your palace

Think of a building that you know the layout of rather well, such as your childhood home. This is a great place to start with this exercise because it is seared into your mind with intimate detail, which gives you more power to build it.

Step Two: Create images

Do you want to learn to better memorize your grocery list? Then create items to later store in your palace that coincide with your list. Remember to use your imagination! The more funny or bizarre, the easier it will be to recall them. Unbelievably the course of evolution itself has hardwired the topics of jokes and sex into our core thinking, which is why many people associate items they need to remember into these two categories the most.

Step 3: Place imagery into your palace

Going back to the grocery list analogy, walk through your childhood household in your mind and place the memorable objects within the house in the order that you need them to be in. If done correctly, you should only have to retrace your steps one to two times to recall what you need to get from the store.

Step 4: Take a stroll in your palace

Once your items are in your mental palace, it is time to take a walk through it to ensure that can recall everything. This strategy does not only have to be used for simple things such as a grocery list. Many lecturers use it to connect points within their speeches. Yes, with this method your mind is going to be filled with a variety of things, from human and animal parts to dinosaurs to other absurdities. Make it fun!

Memory palace example

- *You head into your house and once through the threshold of your front door, you view a cow on fire standing in your entryway. This symbolizes that you need to purchase burgers at the store.*

- *Heading through the hallway, you see that your stairs are wet with the cow's blood. This symbolizes that you need to get ketchup as well.*

- *Once at the top of the stairs, you see large human buttocks, symbolizing that you need to pick up hamburger buns.*

Mind Mapping Process

The process of mind mapping is all about the gathering of your thoughts in a visual format. This helps to ensure that you can embrace things with much more creativity as well as effectiveness. These maps are diagrams that connect you to the information you need to acquire and recall at a later time, whether it is learning about a new topic or obtaining a new skill set. Many professionals use mind mapping to expand their creativity, as well as to connect with others through the means of natural association, which leads to the generation of innovative new ideas faster.

No matter how many notes you take on a subject that you wish to learn about, mind mapping triumphs every time. They can help us see the bigger picture, which makes it easier to grasp and understand it more deeply. They have been proven to assist those to be more efficient, thanks to their ability to quickly judge complex projects much easier. The best part? As new ideas are spun, new paths can be explored! There is no "basic" way to create a mind map. Whether you use pen and paper or embrace technology if it leads you to the right path that is what matters. Just remember to be creative!

Photographic Memory Training Tips

Training to sharpen your memory skills is quite simple. In fact, even a child can learn some of these techniques without too much hassle or effort. These tips will not only help you improve your memory but will also help you be able to recall information at a much quicker rate.

Lessen distractions

Being able to minimize things that distract you is one of the best ways to develop a skill in recalling memory. Do not blame your forgetfulness on memory, but rather turn the blame to the distractions that plague us each day. Do your best to focus on one thing at a time, instead of trying to take on multiple things at once.

Improve your lifestyle

Many memory issues that we face are due to our body's response to anger, depression, anxiety, and other negative feelings. It is important, not only for your recall rate but also for your overall well-being, to keep symptoms that can negatively impact you physically, mentally, and emotionally at bay. Ensure that you spend plenty of time doing things that you love and learn from.

Get moving

Physical activity helps increase the flow of blood to every part of your body, including the brain. Exercise allows those essential nutrients along with more oxygen to reach our brains so that they can perform better! 30 minutes of exercise 5 days a week is plenty. But more is even better.

Activate your brain

Your brain should be considered a muscle; if you don't use it, you will eventually lose it. The more we use it, the better it will perform when we really need it to. Try to incorporate some of these brain-stimulating activities into your daily schedule to get your brain off autopilot and concentrating on something more invigorating:

- o   Learn a new language

- o   Learn how to play an instrument

- o   Perform crossword puzzles

- o   Play a board game

- o   Read the newspaper or a book

Visualization

Visualization can improve your memory retention. Ensure that you practice visualization techniques and use image associations on a regular basis.

Military techniques

There are vital tricks that our own military use while in the line of duty and in combat, such as psychic spying and objective viewing. They can remember coordinates, locations, and images with these techniques, which are essential not only for their survival but their mission and those they are with.

Courses and exercises

There are hundreds of courses and things you can do to improve your memory. This could be from picture games, telling stories, building lists, and word association exercises. These games make it seem like you are not even learning or practicing memory retention and are effective at getting the job done.

Become self-directed

You are the only one that can take control of what you get out of the knowledge you acquire. Ask questions if needed! There are plenty of ways to obtain resources to receive the help you need! The more you inquire, the faster you learn things.

Build your background knowledge

When we take the time and initiative to learn things on our own accord, the more quality of learning improves in the long run.

Create discipline in learning

When you go into your sessions of memory training, you need to go in with a mind clear of all other distractions. Easier said than done, I know. Multi-tasking, no matter how beneficial our society claims it is, is not to be done while undergoing memory sessions. This also means while you are putting your learning curves into practice in real life as well. If your mind is preoccupied, this leaves very little room to conduct a photographic memory session completely. Do not divide up your attention into various sections. Keep your attentive eye on that memorizing prize!

Decide your learning objectives

Whenever you finally get the spark to acquire any new knowledge, it is important to ask yourself why you want to learn this and if it is worth your time and energy. Determine your purpose of learning and practicing something. This way, you will pay better attention and give it more special recognition as you go along.

Memory Strategies

Use image associations

This tip especially comes in handy for attempting to locate something that you cannot find. If you are looking for a book or car keys, take a second to imagine where they would be. If you book is perhaps called "A Hundred Suns," visualize what a hundred of those suns would appear like. Imprinting images within your mind can help you recall the book and perhaps find it later too.

Repetition of names

If you are one that struggles with recalling people's names or names of certain things, you are not the only one. Many people have a hard time retaining names, especially when trying to remember more than one or two names at once.

o   After meeting someone, repeat their name back to them. "It is so nice to meet you 'so-so.' If you did not hear their name correctly or didn't hear quite how they pronounced it, clarify it right then to avoid asking it again later, saving yourself from the embarrassment.

o   Learn to associate newly acquired names with someone you already know with the same name. If you do not know someone personally by that name, think of characters in books or favorite films. This association assists with recalling the names at a later time.

Utilize 'chunking'

Even though this technique sounds more like an issue that your car is having, it is actually a psychological phrase about a memory retention process that involves the clumping together of items, words, numbers, etc. on the same list to ensure you remember them.

o   If attempting to memorize your grocery
    list, put all items into categories, such as
    fruits, veggies, frozen, condiments, meats,
    etc. Or, you can even categorize lists by
    meals you are going to make from the
    items you are trying to memorize.

o   Dividing sets of specific numbers into
    smaller sections will help you recall
    telephone, social security, credit card
    numbers, etc. Instead of trying to
    remember an entire sequence of numbers,
    divide them up into sections. For
    example, instead of 1234567890,
    memorize it as 123-456-7890. This will
    assist you in repeating it back to yourself
    to ensure the proper memorization of it.

Get out those UNO cards

Or any deck of cards, for that matter. Whichever
deck suits your fancy! You will be utilizing them
for a while, so choose wisely. Draw the top three
cards and try to memorize those cards. Then
place those three back into the deck at random
and spread them out. From the spread-out deck,
choose your three cards and put them in the

same order that they were earlier. Perform this exercise with three cards for a week, five the next week, then continue to increase your card count each week. Do this until you have the capability to memorize the entire deck in one sitting.

Domino trick

With a box of dominos make a pattern out of 10 of them. Memorize that pattern. Each week thereafter add 10 more dominos to your pattern. Do so until you can use the entire box. This method takes a while!

Picture engraining

This method is one used by our military to learn names and recognize faces quickly. You must not miss a day, or you have to perform this exercise for another week. You will need:

o A piece of paper that contains a cut-out box the size of 1 paragraph

o A paragraph of words you choose

o A windowless room

o A small but bright light

- Head to your darkroom and set up your light, turn it on and proceed to set up your paragraph so that the hole of your box covers up everything but the paragraph you wish to memorize. Look at the paragraph in front of you for 5 minutes. Turn off the light while you are still staring at the page. Repeat this same process each day for a month or until you can recall the paragraph in its entirety without any mistakes. This process utilizes light to engrain the visual of what you want to memorize into your brain.

Honing your Eidetic Memory Capabilities

Since we have discussed many ways to develop your photographic memory skills, we might as well touch base about a technique you can use to better your eidetic memory skills as well!

Training your brain to memorize in eidetic ways is not complicated, but it must be exercised in three ways: ***speed, space, and quantity***.

Speed

This technique was created to train the speed at which you perceive and remember what you have seen. The idea is to make the amount of time you need to memorize shorter and shorter.

- o Utilize a program on your computer that lets you view something for short periods of time. Show things for 10 seconds to start out. And decrease over time as you grasp the training. People who can memorize at great speeds usually just have to look at things for less than 100 ms to memorize a list of say, around 10 numbers.

Space

The goal of this technique is to exercise the brain to memorize things that are separated by just a space that is big yet small enough for your eyes to visualize and memorize in a single glance. The idea of the space exercise is to memorize things without eye movement.

- o Write down a phone number that you can read in a single eyeshot. Ensure that you are only using your peripheral vision. To really train utilizing this technique a computer program that shows things in a separated way in both height and width is best. Start with shorter distances, gradually working your way up to farther distances while taking in more information.

Quantity

The goal of this technique is to memorize and remember as much information as you possibly can.

o Utilize a computer program that provides you with items to memorize and gradually increase the number of subjects while lessening the time you have to do so. If you do not wish to use a program, writing or typing out telephone numbers is another great way, adding more numbers as you decrease your memorization time.

Chapter 8:
Lifestyle Changes to Improve Your Memory

Back in the good old days of research, it was believed that your brain function peaked during early adulthood and then declined slowly over time, resulting in lapses of memory and experiencing brain fog from time to time throughout the retirement years.

These days, it is well-known that the modern way of life plays a role in our cognitive decline, which is why when we continually expose ourselves to a poor diet, lack of quality sleep, chemicals, toxins, and stress, we are much less likely to use our memory to its full capacity.

When we live a healthier lifestyle, we support our brain health and encourage the growth of neurons. The memory center of your brain, known as the hippocampus, can produce new cells throughout your lifetime, which is what gives your brain the tools it needs to hone your memory skills. These tools are based on the lifestyle you live, which is a great news since it means you can change your daily routine to improve your memory!

Eat better

The foods you consume and don't consume play a vital role in how good your memory is. Fresh vegetables and healthy fats are crucial as you avoid carbohydrates and excess sugars.

- Brainpower foods:

  o *Walnuts, cauliflower, broccoli, celery*, and *curry* have compounds and antioxidants that protect your brain's health and help to produce new cells.

  o *Garbanzo beans, crab, red meats, blueberries*, and *healthy fats* are amazing foods for better brain health.

You also should increase your intake of animal-based omega-3's and reduce your consumption of damaged omega-6 fats that are in items such as vegetable oil.

Exercise

When you get moving, you are encouraging your brain to work at its optimum capacity since it stimulates the nerve cells throughout the body. That allows those cells to multiply, become stronger, and form connections that keep your body and brain from becoming damaged.

It has been proven that those who exercise regularly were able to quickly grow and expand their memory center in the brain by a couple of percent per year.

Quit multitasking

Now more than ever, many of us perform the action of multitasking in all aspects of life; from home, to work, to when we drive, while we eat, etc. The reality is, multitasking slows us down and we are more prone to making errors as we become more forgetful.

Studies have proven that you need at least 8 seconds to truly commit to a piece of information if you wish to place it in your memory. If you are talking on the phone, carrying groceries, putting down your car keys and reading all at once, you are unlikely to remember anything.

The opposite of multitasking is being mindful. This helps everyone to gain a focus that cannot become distracted. Those that practiced mindfulness were found to improve their reading comprehension and expanded their overall memories since they were having to deal with fewer distracting thoughts.

Get quality sleep

Sleep is an action no human being can avoid, for it enhances your memory and allows you to practice and further improve your performance when it comes to learning challenging skills. Each night of sleep should be at least 4 to 6 hours. Otherwise, you could be majorly impacting your ability to think clearly.

Neuroplasticity, the process of brain growth, is the foundation for the way your brain behaves; this controls behavior, memory, and learning, which is fundamental to everyday life. Plasticity can happen when your brain's neurons are stimulated by experiences and information from the outside world. A lack of sleep can inhibit this from ever occurring.

Allow your brain to play

If you fail to challenge your brain with new information, it starts to deteriorate. When you give your brain an appropriate amount of stimulus, you play an essential role in reversing brain degeneration.

This is why 'brain games' are vital to your brain's health and thus your memory. There are websites and mobile applications that you can use in your free time, such as Luminosity.com or Brain HQ. When you sit down to play these games, dedicate at least 20 minutes to them but don't perform the same task for more than 5 to 7 minutes at a time.

Master new skills

When you get involved in meaningful activities that have a purpose, you are stimulating your entire neurological system, which counteracts the effects of stress and reduces the likelihood that you will develop dementia later in life. It also promotes a healthier well-being.

One of the essential factors when it comes to improving your overall brain function is to engage in brand new tasks. The tasks you get involved in need to hold some sort of importance to you or be interesting or meaningful to hold your attention.

Use mnemonic devices

As you have read previously, mnemonic devices can really come in handy when you are trying to do your best to remember pertinent information. They are tools to help you remember words and concepts and involve organizing them in a format that is easy to remember.

- Acronyms

- Chunking

- Rhymes

- Visualizations

Chapter 8: Lifestyle Changes to Improve Your Memory

Making all the above changes to your lifestyle and daily routine will help you to retain a better memory over time as you practice the techniques and tricks you learn throughout this book! Your body is your temple; if you wish to accomplish big things, you need to take care of it. It is your foundation to success in this life!

Chapter 9:
Tricks to Improve Your Memory

I n the age of advanced technology and the broad span of the internet, it can be easy to dismiss memorization that impresses as a skill that is useless. As you have read, however, having a great recall can give you the upper hand in many situations. This chapter will discuss some cool and fun tricks that you can use to further enhance your memory capabilities.

Clench your right hand when learning and your left hand to recall

Seems weird, but there have been several studies to show that this easy trick can greatly improve your short-term memory. When you are learning something new or retaining information you need to recall in the future, all you need to do is clench your right hand into a fist.

Later, when you need to recall what you absorbed earlier, squeeze your left hand into a fist. So far, studies have shown that this handy trick only seems to work its magic in those that are right-handed.

Coordinate new information with a smell

Smells are a proven trigger when it comes to remembering memories, even better than sound. It's application, however, can be a bit tricky to master. It is recommended to coordinate smells from the time you are trying to memorize to when it needs to be recalled.

- For instance, spray a bit of perfume on the back of your hand or on your wrist as you are reading and then use that same perfume during your presentation, speech, or test.

Coordinate postures

It has been shown that if you keep the same position or posture while you are absorbing information and when you recall it, that it is easier to reach those memories.

- Study in one position, such as at an angle with your legs crossed and then remember the answer to a test in that position.

Chew gum

There are a couple of legitimate theories for why chewing gum enhances memory. One is that the act of chewing leads to an increase in your blood flow, which helps the brain stay active as you memorize. The other theory is that chewing gum is an associated action with memories, which makes it easier to gain access to recollections. Pick up a pack of gum before study time!

Use melody

We all know that it is much simpler to recite the lyrics of a song than the words of a boring essay, right? Well, this is where the power of melody comes in handy if you need to ace a test!

There have been many studies to prove that the efficacy of melodies helps with the learning process. It may seem like a ton of additional work, but it is not hard to piggyback melodies that you love as you memorize new information.

Avoid staying up all night to study

Sleep helps to improve your memory and repetition while taking in information in mass forms decreases even immediate memorability. Distributing practices, which means studying for short bursts of time and taking a break, has been proven to be a better method to memorize information than staying up all night the evening before a test to cram.

Your best bet is to not procrastinate until the last minute and study new concepts a little at a time over just a few minutes each day. Use flashcards and other learning apps that are convenient for you to assist!

Use meditation

Buddhists are truly onto something with the whole meditation ritual. Whether you believe it or not, meditating helps to enlighten people. Meditating 4 times each day for as little as 20 minutes helps to increase cognition by as much as 50 percent! Get your Buddha on!

Exercise more

If you find that some of the above suggestions are too tedious for your liking, then you may appreciate a physical approach more. There is a distinct connection between those that exercise on a regular basis to improve cognitive functioning, which includes memory retention. If you are looking to study and lose weight, this is a win-win scenario!

Drink less alcohol

When you abuse alcohol for a long period of time, this can wreak havoc on your overall memory and the ability to retain new information. While a drink every now and then is perfectly fine, if you are drinking to oblivion several times a month, then it pays to drink a bit less.

Use associations

Many of the tricks that help to improve your memory are all centered around one concept, association. We have dealt with involuntary association, such as recalling a smell or sitting in a similar position. Now, let's talk about voluntary associations.

There are some very simplistic voluntary associations. When you are starting to learn a new language, a sweet trick to remember is to associate new words with a word it sounds like in the language you already know. You will find that this makes it much easier to remember new words!

Bundle memories together

Pattern recognition is a great trick when it comes to the recollection of information. If you are trying your best to recall numbers, bundling memories all into one is a great method. If you can group them up in a meaningful way, you will be better able to remember longer strings of numbers.

For example, phone numbers can be split it up into something like 45 80 90 18. You can remember that the year 1945 was when WWII ended, associate 80's with the 80 and 90's with the 90 and the year 1918 is the year that WWI ended. This is better known as 'chunking' of words.

Jot it down

Writing can activate areas of the brain that are known to store most of our retained information, which is why writing things out makes it easier to recall at a later date. If there is something essential that you need to remember, write it down!

Making a physical note and bringing it with you reinforces that information, no matter what circumstance, such as your phone breaking, etc.

Talk it out

While you don't have to perform long monologues to yourself in front of the mirror (but do as you wish!), you are better able to remember things once they are said aloud. In fact, this has been shown to improve accuracy by as much as 15 percent. Talking to yourself has also been shown to make you a smarter human being, so why not turn it into an everyday habit? However, it may be best that you practice this ritual in solitude.

Be mindful

One of the easiest ways to improve your memory is to be more consciously present in your day to day life and pay closer attention to what is being said, taught, and/or shown to you to understand. When you allow your mind to daydream, you fail to form memories and will have issues retrieving that information later.

Visualization

Visualization has been discussed several times in this book so far because it is an amazing way to enhance your overall memory. When you can create images in your mind, you can anchor new information with a symbol, making it much easier to recall.

Use repetition

If you need to remember a certain piece of information, especially a chunk that you find yourself forgetting, then repeat it to yourself, over and over again. This works best for objects, people, and locations and causes the information to become implanted and engrained within your mind.

Find the 'why'

When you totally understand the reason behind the information you are attempting to retain, your mind becomes more intrigued by it, which makes it easier to memorize and use later.

Chapter 10:
The Life of Those That Possess Amazing Memories

You may know somebody who can review recollections without a moment's notice, while then again others may have never known about this cerebrum-controlled superpower. For huge numbers of us, it can be very hard to get a handle on this for the lion's share of us don't tackle this ability to recollect things and occasions in the finest of detail. Since there is little science to move down the likelihood of photographic memory being something that a few people are normally conceived with, while others can endeavor to learn it, it is imperative that we step directly into the shoes of those that claim and have given entirely sufficient confirmation that they have this capacity to see the world in an exceptionally definite organization. This section is brimming with exposures from individuals who have had individual experiences with this territory of their mind, and how this capacity to keep up memory so well has influenced their lives.

There have been numerous endeavors to get portrayals from those that say they can review things at a photographic rate. It is very intriguing to look at each piece of data that individuals can review with no issues. Some can clearly recollect the way something looks or the hints of a specific circumstance while others recall correct discussions verbatim. From the chateaus of a portion of the wealthiest individuals on the planet to those that abide in the filthiest regions of the greatest to littlest urban areas, the enchanted viewpoints that photographic memory brings to the table live in numerous spots here on our planet and in numerous places that we don't anticipate.

The Story of Betty

Betty, who dwells in west Michigan, claims she can imagine individuals, even those that she has looked at for seconds, in strong detail. She can recall subtle elements of the adornments they were wearing, down to what number of pearls or gems. She can review correct haircuts and how

Chapter 10: The Life of Those That Possess Amazing Memories

that specific individual did their make-up that day. She says that out of around eighty to one-hundred individuals she sees once a day between her drive to work and amid her work day, she can review eye-shading and diverse arrangements of garments every one of them tends to wear frequently, and points of interest of tattoos and a few discussions.

While reviewing harder to achieve circumstances in her brain, Betty can really envision herself walking around the scene at which that particular memory occurred. She asserts that it seems as though she sees the world she has officially gathered already from a birds-eye view. Indeed, even encounters and scenes that she dwelled in long, long ago can be gone by if she wishes. She says she discovered comfort in the review school play area back when she was a child, for her youth at home was not all that awesome.

Betty likewise expresses that she can tune in to music without the requirement for a radio, CD player or some other melodic gadget, for she can hear it by memory. The thing is, it now and then makes her crazy to review music along these lines since her psyche plays just a single instrument at any given moment.

Despite the considerable number of advantages that accompany having this apparently unnatural human "superpower", Betty says there are a couple of drawbacks, at any rate from her very own outlook. She cannot control when she envisions recollections. When she hears a specific piece of a specific tune, it triggers her psyche to go into a kind of time twist and influences her to return to the recollections her mind partners with that segment of the melody. Furthermore, with regards to figuring up math conditions or anything including numbers she is in for a psychological. When she is learning new conditions progressively, it triggers her brain to need to imagine different mixes of past lessons. This can make for a hard time focusing on nailing the exercise she is attempting to learn right now.

Even though it sounds astounding to have the capacity to flawlessly review extraordinary and agreeable encounters that she went through with others, it once in a while harms her when cherished one that she imparted those

Chapter 10: The Life of Those That Possess Amazing Memories

encounters to can't review them at all or not close as unmistakably as possible.

How is it for Betty to rest a few evenings? Awful, as she states. There are a few occasions where while she is trying to rest, terrible recollections will fly into her head, making a domino impact over her whole night's rest. She revealed when she sees or hears the voice of Winnie the Pooh, her mind naturally returns to a bad dream that she had when she was a child when the agreeable bear woke up and assaulted her violently.

Just a couple of individuals in Betty's own life think about her psychological capacities with regards to her memory maintenance. What's more, for those that know about her memory capacity, she gets asked: "Why are you not getting extraordinary evaluations on the off chance that you can recollect everything?" Her answer? Photos inside her memory are very divided, making it relatively difficult to assemble while she is trying or reviewing anything. It takes a ton of vitality to really envision one specific memory. She wishes she had significantly more control over her stunning mental and remembering abilities.

The Story of Jill

While a few people may have a light bulb moment when it comes to their capacity to recall, Jill's story is very novel. At the midlife age of her mid-forties, Jill Price is one of the most normally reported people who has expressed and demonstrated her psychological limit with regards to her photographic memory. She has been known as the 'lady who can't overlook.' Wherever she ventures, if there is something inside her surroundings that helps her to remember any kind of life circumstance she has already experienced, she tends to recount an anecdote about those past circumstances with whomever she is with at the time. Ms. Price has been recorded experiencing a one-on-one meeting with the prestigious Diane Sawyer about her memory capacities, that later was shown on the well-known television show, o 20/20. While on air Sawyer solicited Price to review minutes from TV history. She addressed each inquiry with exactness and on the ones that she couldn't review correct, point by point data, she could depict what she was wearing, eating, doing or the climate outside that specific day.

Chapter 10: The Life of Those That Possess Amazing Memories

Until her presentation on 20/20, numerous individuals had not known about Jill Price. Other than her nearby family and companions that were always amazed by her capacity to recollect everything with such exactness, the world was unaware of her. As per Price, while her grand memory framework was exceptional to others, it was sometimes a weight to her, and she needed answers in the matter of how and why her cerebrum worked not quite the same as everybody around her. In June of the year 2000, Price went over a site for a UC Irvine neuroscientist, James McGaugh and sent him a definite email, clarifying her circumstance. To her incredulity, he replied with some distrust. After meeting McGaugh's state of mind toward Price changed rather quickly, as he ran lab work and tests. He knew she was something exceptional. He acquainted Price with his group of specialists, who talked with her over the span of a five-years. The meetings were kept secret until the point that both Price and her new fan club were comfortable telling the general population. In 2006, an article composed by the associates highlighting Price was distributed in the Neurocase diary.

Photographic Memory

When this article was published, Price got offers from the media including Morning Edition. The day she was interviewed by Diane Sawyer for 20/20 the interview was taped for the following day's show of Good Morning America.

Prices' story, regardless of numerous faultfinders along her ride to the popularity she has gotten, is famously genuine. She has amazed a lot of people in her and has since spread her story to others, particularly the parts in which she has battled with her capacity. "There is a great deal of drawbacks with regards to keeping everything composed in my mind and reviewing it to others. Some days are dim and forlorn. There are days where I solidify up and can't review a solitary memory from my whole lifetime. Thank heavens that only keep going a couple of minutes. There are some days that I am anxious about the possibility that I will lose my great blessing for eternity. Also, there are some days I feel objectified for science and has a diversion for others. My experience turning out about my psychological capacities beyond any doubt has given me understanding with respect to how to appropriately deal with my blessing, and who acknowledges me for me". Since Price, nobody has come across anyone else with her valuable photographic memory abilities.

The Story of Andy

Much the same as each person on the planet, every one of us is exceptionally extraordinary in our own way. The same goes for how our brains hold and in the end review data. Andy's story is comparable to Betty and Jill's. He claims to have a remarkable memory, however just specific regions, particularly those with respect to examples and courses. He expresses that he can review examples and requests of things like groupings of numbers and word phrases. This goes for certain symbolism too. He additionally says that he can without a doubt recall specifics with overwhelming point of interest, portraying things down to the column of a sweater in which a string was adrift.

In Andy's school, he is notable for remembering expansive talks for class and discussing dates and conditions. At whatever point his t companions go on long excursions, they never bring along the GPS if Andy has been to those spots since he can review road signs and recall correct turns.

Even though Andy likes his normal blessing, he needs to get a couple of things clear to those that are interested in how the psyches of individuals with incredible memory abilities work. Above all else, having higher memory maintenance does not make those individuals smarter than those with normal capacities with regards to memory. Despite the fact that they can recollect essential things for critical occasions, this does not mean they fundamentally comprehend what they have retained or recalled. For Andy specifically, remembering blends of numbers and letters is truly something he does to translate math conditions, entangled discourses, and different readings. He feels that his method for absorbing data is not the same as different children his age. He has figured out how to legitimately store every one of the parts of the data he obtains in the correct spots to filter through them at a later time.

He alludes to his capacity to remember things as a non-advanced rendition of a document framework. Despite the fact that Andy can inform somebody regarding a specific timeframe in relatively correct detail, if asked, this does not mean he can do so immediately without fail. "The data is there, it just sets aside some opportunity to recover it. It resembles some other normal human cerebrum, yet it is about how you store and sort out all the data we get on an everyday premise." Andy says that if a specific date was more critical to him, more subtle elements emerge to him more rapidly than unexceptional days where his mind did not feel the need to retain everything in his environment.

"Indeed, even those like me need to recollect that we are just as human and that regardless of how hard we attempt to hold everything, we are as yet going to overlook a few things."

As an understudy, Andy has taken in the most difficult way possible that liquor incredibly restrains his capacity to recall occasions and review things that he took in the night prior to a major gathering over an end of the week. He tells individuals that anybody can practice their cerebrum, it is about the amount you truly need to learn in a lifetime.

Conclusion

I want to congratulate you on making it to the end of *Photographic Memory*! Now, it is time for a quiz!

Just kidding, no quiz today, but once you begin to learn and harness the power of the memory-enhancing strategies in this book, perhaps I will have a test for you to conquer by then!

As you have learned, photographic memory may not be as possible as it is for those in the Hollywood movies, but improving your memory is very possible with the help of brain strengthening techniques, a healthier lifestyle, and the willpower to learn!

I challenge you to begin learning at least one of the methods you found to be the most intriguing to you in this book once you put it down. What do you have to lose? We could all greatly benefit from enhancing our brains power to recall information and events. As soon as next month you can be living a life in better clarity than you have ever before in your life!

I hope that this book was fun to read and able to provide you with the tools you need to achieve brain-powered success!